Ruining the New Road

William Matthews

Cooper Dillon

Copyright © 1967-1970, 2011
by The Estate of William Matthews
All rights reserved
First edition (Reprint)

Cooper Dillon Books
San Diego, California
CooperDillon.com

Cover Art & Design: Max Xiantu

ISBN-10: 0-9841928-5-9
ISBN-13: 978-0-9841928-5-4

Printed in the United States

Some of these poems first appeard in the following publications, whose editors are thanked: Apple, Café Solo, Cloud Marauder, The Dragonfly, kayak, Kumquat, Lillabulero, Minnesota Review, The Nation, Panama Gold, Poetry Northwest, Quarterly Reivew of Literature, Red Cedar Review, Shenandoah, Souther Poetry Review, Tennessee Poetry Journal.

A portion of this manuscript appeared in Search Party: Collcted Poems, Edited by Sebastian Matthews & Stanley Plumly *(Mariner Books/ Houghton Mifflin Company).*

Special thanks to Steve Mooney.

This book is for Marie.

Table of Contents

The Search Party	3

I

Suddenly	7
Der Doppelgänger	8
Cuckold	9
March Heat	10
Psychoanalysis	11
The Asian War	12
Washington, D.C., During the Asian War	13
Blues for John Coltrane, Dead at 41	14
Coleman Hawkins (d. 1969), RIP	15
Newark under Martial Law	16
School	17
Leaving Mexico City	18
Nothing but Bad News in the Paper	19
My Routine	20
Replacing the Director	21
Jealousy	22
Oh No	24

II

Moving	27
Lust	28
Holding the Fort	29
Faith of Our Fathers	30
Why We Are Truly a Nation	31

You Too	32
The Summer Night You Can't Forget	33
The Poem about Insomnia	34
On Cape Cod a Child Is Stolen	35
Driving All Night	36
Just Before Waking,	
We Dream of Each Other	37
Hello, Hello	38
Please	39
Thursday Morning	40
My Love of the Lioness	41
Oh Yes	43

III

Old Girlfriends	47
Continuo	48
What You Need	49
How to Die	50
Swimming off Cape Hatteras	51
What to Do with the Morning Paper	52
La Pourriture Nobel Sets in at	
Château d' Yquem	53
Wehlener Sonnenuhr Auslese 1959	54
Good Night	55
Our Song	56
Cayuga Lake in Winter	57
January Thaw	60
Help	61
Good Night Again	62
Yes!	63

"I write for the same reason I live: for love, the pleasure of work, the continual need to understand the world and be at the same time in it. The earth has its own orders, lovely and harrowing, and I would like to show them. The poems are the records of that continuing attempt."

–Bill Matthews

Ruining the New Road

William Matthews

The Search Party

*I wondered if the others felt
as heroic
and as safe:* my *unmangled family
slept while I slid uncertain feet ahead
behind my flashlight's beam.
Stones, thick roots as twisted as
a ruined body,
what did I fear?
I hoped my batteries
had eight more lives
than the lost child.
I feared I'd find something.*

*Reader, by now you must be sure
you know just where we are,
deep in symbolic woods.
Irony, self-accusation,
someone else's suffering.
The search is that of art.*

*You're wrong, though it's
an intelligent mistake.
There was a real lost child.
I don't want to swaddle it
in metaphor.
I'm just a journalist
who can't believe in objectivity.
I'm in these poems
because I'm in my life.
But I digress.*

*A man four volunteers
to the left of me
made the discovery.*

*We circled in like waves
returning to the parent shock.
You've read this far, you might as well
have been there too. Your eyes accuse
me of false chase. Come off it,
you're the one who thought it wouldn't
matter what we found.
Though we came with lights
and tongues thick in our heads,
the issue was a human life.
The child was still
alive. Admit you're glad.*

I

Suddenly

The truth is out, and nothing
is the same. You are
the last surprise, I am
an elk come too far south,
puzzled by villages.
Too late, too late, I run
through snowy fields
on melting legs.

Der Doppelgänger

1. Pale Fire

In sleep we issue from the earth
like prayers the nuns have swallowed
but can't keep down.
The dead skins of our names
fall from our lips.
We begin
talking to ourselves in tongues.

2. Reconnaissance

Not a soul nor a mind
but another body
rises from the sleeping body.
The night falls away from it
as water before a ship's prow,
lights and cries staining the silence
it glides across.
The body, the magical body
stuffed with rich burdens.

3. Rising

When I wake up, who knows
what I learned sleeping?
Somebody lifts two pennies off
and I come back on mossy feet
to slip in through the open eyes.

Cuckold

You can hear the silverware
catching its eager breath
inside the sleeping drawer.
It is waiting to elope.

When you lean to the appliances
they make the noise you hear
when you get to the phone too late.

That empty bottle of Schlitz
belonged to someone
earlier tonight.
Just now his drowsy breath
coils from the bottle
and moves out into the room
with you.

You move inside your fear
like an old priest
saying Mass alone before dawn.
At the right moments
your arms stretch out and legs bend down,
imagining the bells.

March Heat

At night the wind dies
like a settling canvas.

Under a clotted sky
complaints swarm at great distances,
their slow wings beating.

From their windows
tenants lean out,
ladling the thick air in.

Nothing can ease the March heat
nor make it stay.

Psychoanalysis

Everything is
luxurious; there is no past,
only an oceanic present.
You troll along in your glass-
bottomed boat.
Parents and siblings lurk
among the coral with thick eyes,
they will not eat you
if you understand them
well enough. Stop,
you whisper to the ingratiating
pilot, here we are,
maybe this means an end
to all those hours listlessly improvising.
Letting down
the line you think maybe
now you have it,
it will come up slick
with significance, laden
with the sweet guilt you can name.

The Asian War

We talk about it
clinically, as if it were
a mold the body couldn't
shed. We've lost control.
Our fingers thicken,
growing a hot clumsy crust
until they are as stiff
as icicles and we drop
everything, leaflets,
bombs, all hope.

Washington, D.C., During the Asian War

Every century or so
a public building sifts
into itself
like a grain settling in a silo.

Here no blood
bristles in the wrist;
we sleep as cozily
as relics in an alter.

This is the sunken city.
Here aqualungs explode
like milkweed pods
and no one goes away.

Blues for John Coltrane, Dead at 41

Althought my house floats on a lawn
as plush as a starlet's body
and my sons sleep easily,
I think of death's salmon breath
leaping back up the saxophone
with its wet kiss.

Hearing him dead,
I feel it in my feet
as if the house were rocked
by waves from a soundless speedboat
planing by, full throttle.

Coleman Hawkins (d. 1969), RIP

As if that sax
were made of bone wrenched from his wrist
he urged through it dank music
of his breath. When he blew ballads
you knew one use of force:
witholding it.
This was a river of muscles.
Old dimes oily from handling,
eggs scrambled just right in a diner
after eight gigs in nine nights,
a *New Yorker* profile, a new Leica
for the fun of having one.
Gasps and twitches.
It's like having the breath
knocked out of me
and wearing the lost air for a leash.
I snuffle home.
I hate it that he's dead.

Newark under Martial Law

Suburbs ring Newark
like camping Conestogas
but the Indians are inside.
The swooning sentries clutch their knees,
men out in a blizzard
who give up and sleep.
They dream hatred of badgers,
dreams of nosing downward into soil.
At the campfire
each man's hatred is erect.
Night extends as thinly
as an unwound cymbal.
If someone taps it,
eardrums will collapse for miles,
storefronts in a sonic boom.

School

Who was the last English king
to die by violence?
Hands clamor, Let me Let me
kill Charles I.
I bring my tongue down hard.
We gleam, our eyes the color
of the robes the saved put on.
We know everything.

Leaving Mexico City

The 727 trembles
on the runway
like Cortez just come
over the rise, gorging

his eyes.
His men forgot
the shed armor & dead horses
deserted in the jungles.

They scuttled down
like ants along a skeleton.
Later, fleeing town at night
on roads the Aztecs built

painfully across the lake,
they felt their feet
wanting to fold
into the fuselage.

Nothing but Bad News in the Paper

A nervous sentry,
I peer out from the porch.
Thank God you're safe in bed.
Rumors of sabotage are in the air.

At borders armies gather
and scan for enemies.
Governments rise and fall
like coeds' reputations.
Everywhere life is ludicrous
but absolutely crucial.

I stand on my porch,
a grenade stuck in my throat.

When it explodes
I am blown everywhere.
Even beside
the startled Panamanian
sifts down some skin
in shreds,
your name written on each
in a clear hand.

My Routine

All day I sit like some rigid
aging Indian,
sick of moral victory.
Love, my magic bean,
I cannot bury you.
Nights I go groggy with lust:
I can almost feel your tongue,
that candle, at my ear.
No no
it's useless,
one may be dazzled
as deer by carlights are.
You are my trance,
you bitch, my clarity of fever.
When I close my eyes
I pull a blanket
of ashes over them.

Replacing the Director

Because the movie will
not force me to believe it,
I leave my body in its twelfth-row seat
and stand inside a circle
of technicians by the lake,
quieting them.
Filming begins.
Beautifully out of focus,
as I asked,
Jeanne Moreau's face
floats up like a discarded dress.
I watch the man who plays my part
bend to kiss her.
Playing love scenes, it's hard
not to become aroused.
Take her, I tell myself. He does.

Jealousy

1.

Now I have this smoking coal
I'm growing from carbon
in my gut,
a snake hoping to sleep off
his meal of fire.
My heart enters a half-life
of sludged pumping.

2.

This lump, this pearl I am making
sometimes jumps
                like a burning bee.
Black honey!

3.

This way love dies
                somewhere else,
like an arm wriggled out of its sling.

4.

If I rasp like a crashing plane,
like a ground-down spine
made into a rhythm instrument,
it is beacuse I am knitting
a fern of bone for your thigh,

Oh
    I wish it were so,
I'd take my stubbled tongue
and file these words
            down
to their nub of curse.

5.

In the dewy grass, first July light,
I blurt damp balls of breath up,
suck them back in.
            Well hell
I shall be warm
by my own fire
though the sun come.

Oh No

All this noisy profundity,
this joyful pain,
what has it meant?

In me the rapist
lives a second life just
as he lived his first
except he plans it better.

Still my body
is a bag of broken secrets.

II

Moving

When we spurt off
in the invalid Volvo
flying its pennant of blue fumes,
the neighbors group and watch.
We twist away like a released balloon.

Lust

It is a squad car idling
through my eyes, bored,
looking for a crime to crush.
Two tough cops drive it,
three years on the same beat,
sick of each other.
To it I am no better
than a radish.
I hear its indolent engine
grump along in second gear,
feel both cops watch me
walk with stiff ankles,
a nun among drunks.

Holding the Fort

At first I feel my arms
go off to rest.
They loop off the bed's end
and crawl away, loud
with relief. The legs
go next
and always hunt in pairs.

Only the brain
is left, tiny
in the vast bed.

Outside, the elms lean
into clumps, gossiping
of violence.
Somewhere blood leaks out
from its shocked skin.

Now there's no hope of sleep.
Under the sheets
my absent body tingles
like an amputated toe.

Faith of Our Fathers

Now it is time to see what's left:
not much.
Gulls above the scrub pine, the tufted dunes—
though nothing visible emits that low, slurred moan—,
the graves in rows like a tray full of type.
What we have lost
you may guess by what we have kept.
We rise to sing
like beach grass swaying in the wind.
O hymn of salt, the pages of the hymnal
riffling, turning
at last by themselves.

Why We Are Truly a Nation

Because we rage inside
the old boundaries,
like a young girl leaving the Church,
scared of her parents.

Because we all dream of saving
the shaggy, dung-caked buffalo,
shielding the heard with our bodies.

Because grief unites us,
like the locked antlers of moose
who die on their knees in pairs.

You Too

A dishonored woman curdles milk.
So she mumbles the old prayer:
Louise Louise, God love you too.
The slurred words drop in beads
from her bruised lips. Yes
rosaries of lilt, yes
thorns of flesh!
I kiss each wrinkled heel Louise,
twin lizards. I pry the faded cotton B-cup goblets
from your breasts, barnbreath
and loam, rope thighs,
I drink from your silt grotto.
Yes harsh hair
and hayflecks on your neck
God love you too
bright spike of fire.

The Summer Night You Can't Forget

Lull, the deep gauzy lull
of a boat in its cove.

The grass tickles her belly,
her ankles flutter;
she wants her lust as perfect
as a prince at his coronation.
Like huge stallions
bearing the heralds,
her thighs quiver in place.
When is the precise time
to turn over?

Her clothes thrum from her
in a flock,
a roar in the crowd's throat.

She is beautiful.
She writhes in the damp grass
like light reflected
in an emerald.
There's no way
you can own such loveliness.
It lives in its skin
like a worm
in the earth.

The Poem about Insomnia

Again,
like the wretched lover
taking off his clothes again,
I try to write
the poem about insomnia,
shining my broken light.

But my hands unravel.
Perhaps the poem
is really about sleep.

From boxes crammed with dreams
crinoline fears float up
like dandelion tufts.
We spread a huge white wispy picnic cloth.
They read to me in turn.

On Cape Cod a Child Is Stolen

Fog has sealed in the house
like a ship in a bottle.
All the people of the house
are dreaming of his future;
only the Puritans
and he aren't sleeping.
They watch him lie too long in bed,
the fog's moist nose at his ear.
Now the muzzle pokes his tiny mouth,
prying it open. They love him;
he's in danger; but it's too late.
His perfect body is still there
but clearly empty. The fog
rolls back to its own place
and the fisherman scrape back
from breakfast and go out to work.

Driving All Night

My complicated past is an anthology,
a long line painted on the plains.
I feel like literary history
about to startle the professors.

But it's not true.

Days ahead, snow heaps up
in the mountains
like undelivered mail.
After driving all night
I guess what it's like
to fly over them.
For the first time you see
how close things are together,
how the foothills push up
just past where you quit
driving. Urgencies
sputter in the exaltation
of chill air.

      Your heart
begins to fall like snow
inside a paperweight.
Oh when in your long damn life,
I ask myself, when will
you seek not a truce,
but peace?

Just Before Waking, We Dream of Each Other

There is no night longer
than this: eyelids
stick shut with plans
for running off to Venice.

I bob in the gondola
of your thighs.
In your version
I am the Doge's servant
who is really a prince.

When you come
to the Doge's ball
we waltz in the pantry
until our knees collapse.

Hello, Hello

All night I wore the phone, a dead scarf,
charred bone of a bishop's mistress.
There was a drone, as if a distant lawn
were being mown.
And I was dying, dying upwards
like pines in a dense grove.
And all I had were these words;
put them down a slot
and they ring like flattened bells,
discs of doused fire.
Come home, come home,
my lungs are thick with the smoke of your absence.

Please

My shoulders stiffen when I think of you.
But your hands pierce them
like a body entering the water.
Always put your gloves
of ashes on before you knock.

Thursday Morning

The dog's been in the garbage
again.
You tighten the fist of your face.
The snowy lawn is pocked
with fragments of a Froot Loops box.
The dog is dazed with winter
light and snow.
Blear, blear,
we're sick of it. Together
we throw the morning over
our left shoulders,
one rhythm, we love each
other so well in our shawls of salt.

My Love of the Lioness

When I think of her shaggy ease,
her stolid redolent musk,
a tongue in my stomach talks.

And she unfurls to her feet
and paces
and her tail waves
like a snake growing out of a ship.
And her toenails click in her cage.

How can I know
what I look at?
Me, with my muscles that knot
like vowels from another language;
me, rationalized and hairless,
a swimmer who shaves his body
for the race.
Me, the maker
of false comparisons,
the lighthouse that never looks in.
I only spin.

And she subsides, the drizzle
and mist of a fountain
that turns itself off for the night.
And I know, watching her sink
into herself,
I know I've locked her up
to symbolize:

her feet as fat as my knees,
pacing, turning that wheel
in her shoulder
at either end of the cage.

Oh Yes

My hands, my fists, my small bells
of exact joy,
clappers cut out
because they have lied.

And your tongue:
like a burnt string
it holds its shape until
you try to lift it.

We're sewn into each other
like money in a miser's coat.
Don't cry. Your wounds are
beautiful if you'll love mine.

III

Old Girlfriends

I thrust my impudent
cock into them
like a hand raised in class.

What they knew that I didn't learn
was not to ask:

one participates.

To say one is "in love"
says everything:
the tongue depressor breaks
into flame.

To say "one" is in love
means me, hero of all these poems,
in love as in a well
I am the water of.

Continuo

It's the chant of the priests
you can't believe
though your knees hurt from not praying.
Your cock crooks over
like a question mark.
Your life is very moving
but it isn't going anywhere.
Your rugs roll up to sleep.

It's an old song you can't recall
about the hearts of men.
Yours is a muscle.

It's the voice of the Greek
who lisped in your wife's ear
all party long—when you got home
her underpants were slick,
her body sang in its sleep.

It's one gift
or another you don't want.
Or could it be
you've held yourself
like a shell to your ear?

Secrets are setting smoky fires
under your tongue.
That musical dial tone
may be your own hushed voice
plotting something you can almost
hear. We'll have to live in fear.

What You Need

Suppose you want to leave your life,
that old ring in the tub,
behind?

It closes cozily
as a clerk's hand,
a coin with fingers.

You hate it
the same way the drunken son
loves Mother.

You will need pain
heaving under you
like frost ruining the new road.

How to Die

You aren't surprised.
You take in water, you lie in the sun.

As warped as an old plank,
you split along the grain.

Swimming off Cape Hatteras

After an inland winter
my flesh falls off
like the glad lover's underwear.

Safely among the netting bones
my blood swims with the sea.

What to Do with the Morning Paper

Details of violence,
the doomsday drum,
news that on icy hills
cars secede from the slopes.
At last, the Celtics succumb.
Pamphlets that explain
French kissing, 50¢
c/o this newspaper.
Stupefaction
crosses Dagwood's brow
in a slow mush,
the wise huskies
winking to each other.

Oyez Oyez
knees love the prints
they leave in the snow,
the sweet pressing
even the snow enjoys.

Kneel in the new hollow
and start a fire.

La Pourriture Noble Sets in at Château d' Yquem

> *Harvest does not begin until the grapes have shrivelled on the vine, the grape water dried out by the late autumn sun. At this stage the bacteria on the skin of the grape go to work, and the grapes rot. In Sauternes this is called* pourriture nobel, *or noble rot, cused by the mold* Botrytis cinerea, *which gives the wine its sweetness and its high alcoholic content.*
> Alexis Lichine,
> The Wines of France

September:
        a thrall
comes into the vines
like frogmen who cut the net
that guards the harbor.

October:
whole villages inside the grapes
drift in the sleep
of saints who feel the wings
lift under them.

November:
        the gathering
of brokers, of buyers,
their mouths dry with risk.

Quick! timing is everything.
The shrunken grapes are choked
with dusty mold.

We hear the polishing of tables,
the leaping molecules
in the stems of the crystal.

Wehlener Sonnenuhr Auslese 1959

for Dave Curry

After each rain the workers
bring the eroded soil
back up the slope in baskets.
When the freezing ground heaves
rocks up, they are gathered,
shattered, the pieces
strewn among the vines.
The sun reflects from them.
In the Moselle the sun
is a broken bottle of light,
same color as the wine.
When you drink it,
you pass through your body
a beloved piece of earth.
You are like the worm,
except you know it.
A door in the earth opens
and you go in, as guest.

Good Night

I sneak into my sons' room
to hear them breathe,
the hum of their intricate
bodies using air.

In her sleep my wife
has pushed away the covers.
Her nightgown is above her waist.
She has burrowed up
like a worm sensing rain.

None of these things is mine!
If I left them out overnight
I would not rust. Now I can lock
the door, turn out lights,
go to bed.
When I calm down and sleep
I dream that the earth beneath the house
is an old ship,
creaking spars and swollen hullgrain,
drifting in new waters.

Our Song

And when you shake your colonies of hair,
you are a willow of bellropes.
All who have loved you clang:
a treeful of musical bruises.
It gives you something to hum,
an anthem, falling asleep.

Cayuga Lake in Winter

1.

The stones in the chill slick slime
are signed by trilobites,
the fish make a dank music
living the winter out.
Talk about cold comfort.
Blood quickened, ears brittle,
I pace the shore
in despair of such patience.
The lake is visible
through fog for twenty yards
but is implied forever,
its breathy
stench of palpable damp.
Matthews you stiff
the frogs clambered out of these waters,
dragging their capes of moss.
What do you make of that?
Turning away,
dragging my sullen feet,
I make a map.

2.

In a stunned sleep
I wake to the lake's sources,
a granular mire
raked by the glacier.
I fold back into the muck
like a fern in reverse.
On either side
toad inhales,
root reaches out,
like roads making a map
the languorous spiders loop
through the cross-haired air.
This is no tickle of connections,
Matthews,
everything stinks of risk.

3.

Next day
I dwindle the lake
to a fact
and call my silly name,
no answer,
a thorn in the ear.
I push myself at the landscape
like a stake.
Now I know to eat my shoes
and bump home on my belly,
proud without pants.
Maps be damned
and to hell with Matthews
too,
that sniveling lyrical
son of a panfish.
I'll scrape home, light a fire,
love my woman
and curse the lies I have lived by.

January Thaw

I slog home:
it's like walking on wet bread.
The dog's breath is a reek
of field mouse
fooled by the early ooze.
Yesterday I said be like the worm,
eat as you go.
Today
a stone lion with pure water pouring
out the mouth.
And the house lists into the night,
a shoulder stuck sleeping in the muck.
Thank God.

Help

for R.B.

A brother dead, an old friend crazed.
The tongue lies broken by short words.
To such mouths
despair uncovers a swollen breast.
Under taut skin,
like flaws in marble:
threads leading back to the snow-eaters,
thin blue veins.
Through them hot blood, the body's lava,
rattles its fragile chain.
Nothing worth learning can be taught
except by example.
We die.
The pronouns frazzle.
We hunt with animals' bones
and learn love from each other.

Good Night Again

You rise,
steam from a kettle.
The sluggish fish
mean business in the lake,
they have no shoulders.
Wake up dear,
the air is clear
as a mirror.

Good days I breathe back
at the coffee,
I swim through the snow
like a boot with gills.
Because you have wrenched my thigh
I limp beside the lake, all day,
with a lilt.

At night, a rasp of snow,
I fall on you.
May we be comfort
and pleasure, one for the other.
We rock a rut
in the road to sleep.

Yes!

You come home loved and troubled,
tired,
and lay your body down before me
like new bread.
It is the same body I have always loved,
and in it your eyes shine
like light still traveling from a dead star.
I give you my love to use
and shake with fear you can't.
A sleep like a long swim
and dreams of things growing,
shuddering, wrenched,
giant kelp 100 ft. high in the ocean,
sage and yarrow,
the ferny lace of hair
around your cunt, marrow
in mending bones.
There is no way to stop growing.
Sleep is a simple faith.
I wake, wanting
the moist pull into you,
your face easing,
love growing in sweet violence.
And then you wake,
still tired, tentative
but languorous.
I know that love is life's best work.

William Matthews was born in Cincinati in 1942. He studied at Yale and the University of North Carolina at Chapel Hill where, with two friends, he founded Lillabulero Press and its poetry magainze, *Lillabulero*. During his lifetime he published eleven books of poetry, including *Time & Money* (1996), which won the National Book Critics Circle Award; *Selected Poems and Translations 1969-1991* (1992); *Blues If You Want* (1989); *A Happy Childhood* (1984); *Rising and Falling* (1979); *Sticks and Stones* (1975); and *Ruining the New Road* (1970). Collections published posthumously include *Search Party: Collected Poems*, edited by his son Sebastian Matthews and Stanley Plumly (2004), *After All: Last Poems* (1998), and *New Hope for the Dead* (2010). He was also the author of a book of essays entitled *Curiosities* (1989).

William Matthews served as president of The Associated Writing Programs and of the Poetry Society of America, and as a member and chair of the Literature Panel of the National Endowment for the Arts. He received fellowships from the Guggenheim and Ingram Merrill foundations, the National Endowment for the Arts, and the Lila Wallace-Reader's Digest Fund, and in April 1997 he was awarded the Ruth Lilly Prize. He taught at numerous schools, including, in his last years, the City College of New York. William Matthews died of a heart attack on November 12, 1997, the day after his fifty-fifth birthday.

www.ingramcontent.com/pod-product-compliance
Lightning Source LLC
Chambersburg PA
CBHW020627300426
44112CB00010B/1227